Impressum
Verlag: BABADADA GmbH, Nedderfeld 112 , 22529 Hamburg
Geschäftsführer / Verlagsleitung: Harald Hof
Druck: Books on Demand GmbH, In de Tarpen 42, 22848 Norderstedt

Imprint
Publisher: BABADADA GmbH, Nedderfeld 112 , 22529 Hamburg, Germany
Managing Director / Publishing direction: Harald Hof
Print: Books on Demand GmbH, In de Tarpen 42, 22848 Norderstedt

School

school

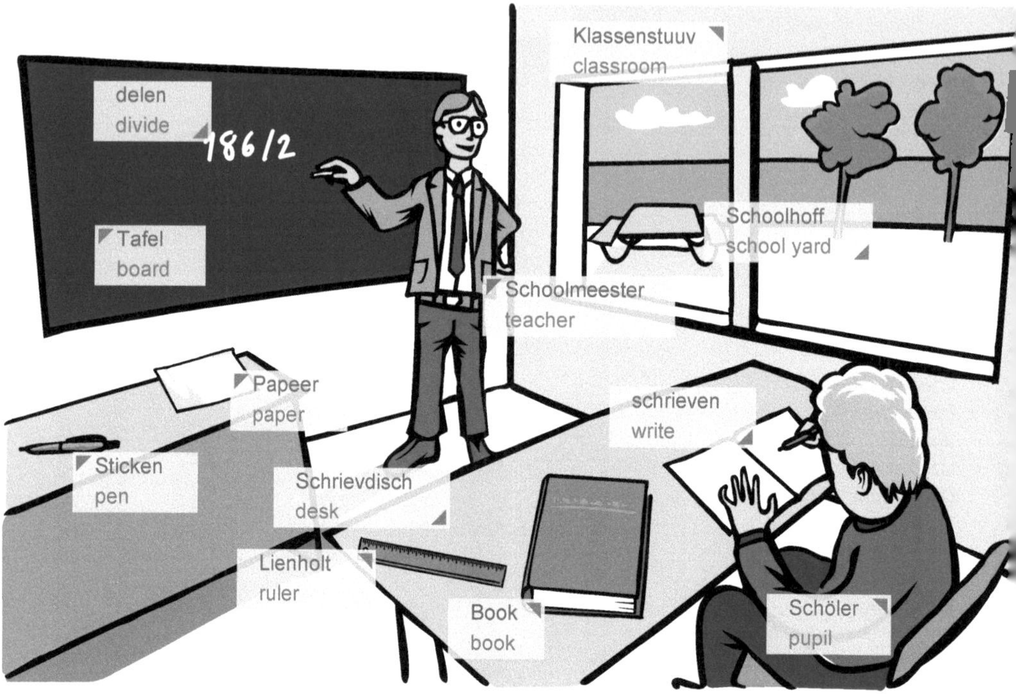

Klassenstuuv
classroom
delen
divide
186/2
Tafel
board
Schoolhoff
school yard
Schoolmeester
teacher
Papeer
paper
schrieven
write
Sticken
pen
Schrievdisch
desk
Lienholt
ruler
Book
book
Schöler
pupil

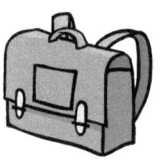

Ranzel

satchel

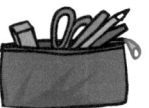

Feddermapp

pencil case

Bleesticken

pencil

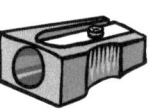

Scharpmaker

pencil sharpener

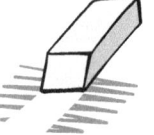

Radeergummi

rubber

Tekenblock

drawing pad

Teken

drawing

Pinsel

paintbrush

Malkassen

paint box

Scheer

scissors

Klever

glue

Heft to'n Öven

exercise book

Huusopgaav

homework

12

Tall

number

2+2

tohooptellen

add

5-2

aftrecken

subtract

2×2

malnehmen

multiply

reken

calculate

A

Bookstaav

letter

ABCDEFG HIJKLMN OPQRSTU VWXYZ

ABC

alphabet

hello

Woort

word

Text

text

lesen

read

Kried

chalk

Stunn

lesson

Klassenbook

register

Pröven

examination

Tüügnis

certificate

Schooluniform

school uniform

Utbillen

education

Nakieksel

encyclopedia

Universität

university

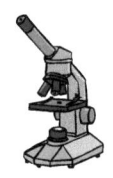

Mikroskop

microscope

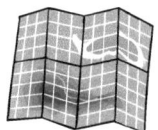

Koort

map

Papeerkorf

waste-paper basket

Törn
travel

Hotel
hotel
Grand
Harbarg
hostel
ROOMS
Wesselstuuv
currency exchange office
Kuffer
suitcase
Auto
car

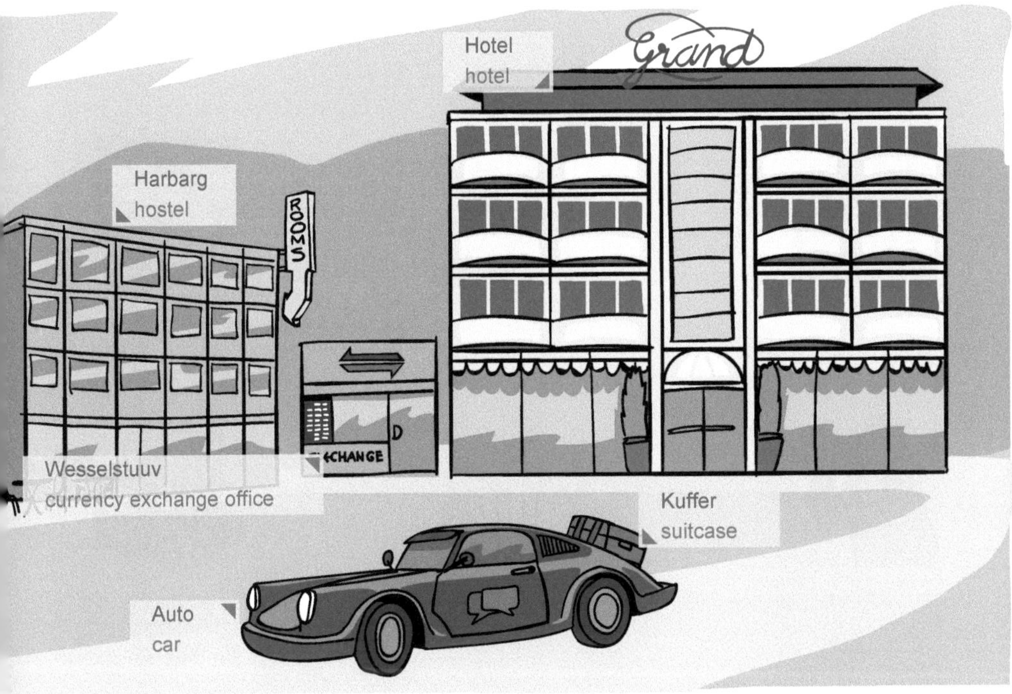

Spraak

language

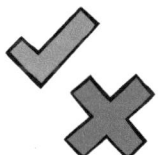

jo / ne

yes / no

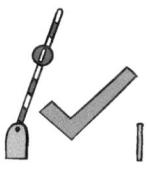

Jo

Okay

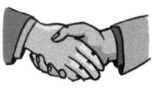

Moin

hello

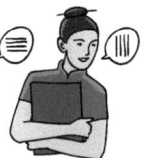

Översetter

translator

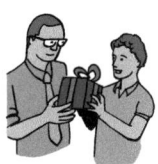

Dank ok

Thank you

Wat kost...?
how much is...?

Ik verstah nich
I don´t get it

Problem
problem

Goden Avend
Good evening!

Moin!
Good morning!

Gode Nacht!
Good night!

Tschüüs
goodbye

Richt
direction

Bagaasch
luggage

Tasch
bag

Rüchsack
backpack

Gast
guest

Stuuv
room

Slaapsack
sleeping bag

Telt
tent

Touristeninformatschoon

tourist information

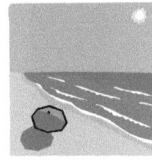

Strand

beach

Kreditkoort

credit card

Fröhstück

breakfast

Meddageten

lunch

Avendeten

dinner

Fohrkort

Ticket

Fohrstohl

elevator

Breefmark

stamp

Grenz

border

Toll

customs

Bottschop

embassy

Visum

visa

Pass

passport

Transport
transport

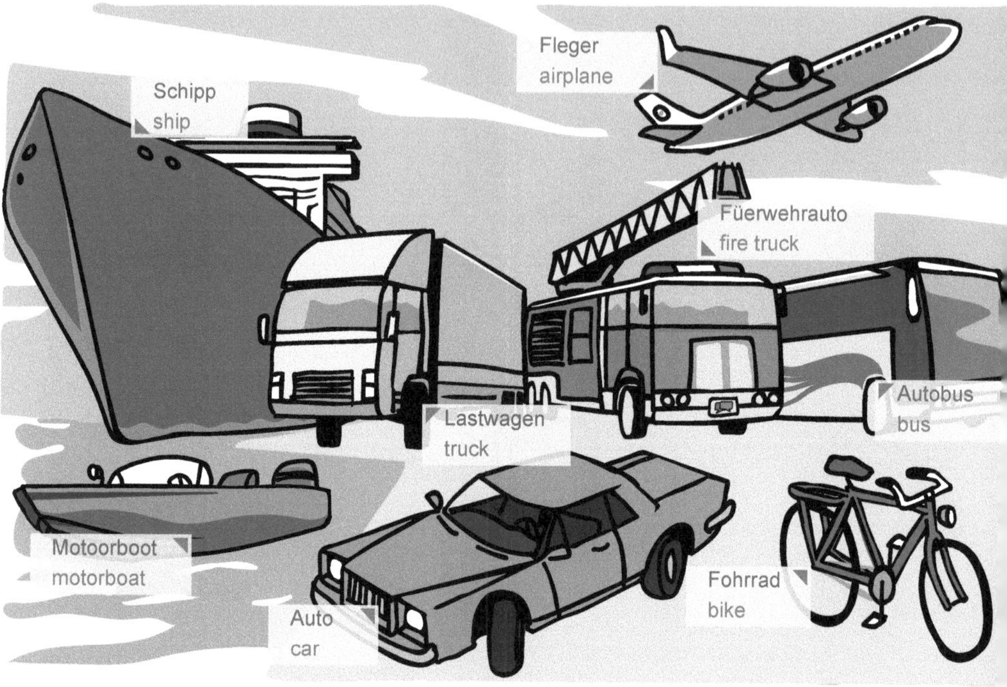
Fleger
airplane
Schipp
ship
Füerwehrauto
fire truck
Autobus
bus
Lastwagen
truck
Motoorboot
motorboat
Fohrrad
bike
Auto
car

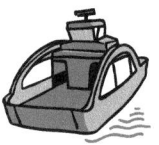

Fähr

ferry

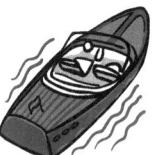

Boot

boat

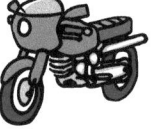

Motoorrad

motorbike

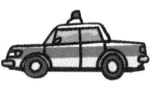

Polizeiauto

police car

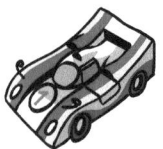

Rönnauto

racing car

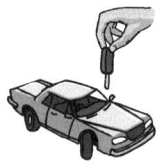

Lehnwagen

rental car

Carsharing

car sharing

Afsleepwagen

tow truck

Müllauto

garbage truck

Motoor

engine

Kraftstoff

fuel

Tanksteed

fuel station

Verkehrsschild

traffic sign

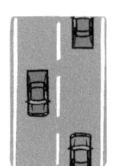

Verkehr

traffic

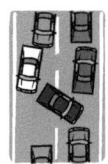

Stau

traffic jam

Afstellplatz

parking lot

Bahnhoff

train station

Sporen

tracks

Tog

train

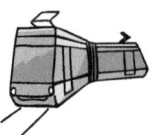

Stratenbahn

tram

Wagon

wagon

Dwarsmöhl

helicopter

Flooghaven

airport

Tower

tower

Fohrgast

passenger

Grootkist

container

Karton

carton

Koor

cart

Korf

basket

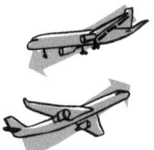

starten / lannen

take off / land

Stadt
city

Dörp

village

Binnenstadt

city center

Huus

house

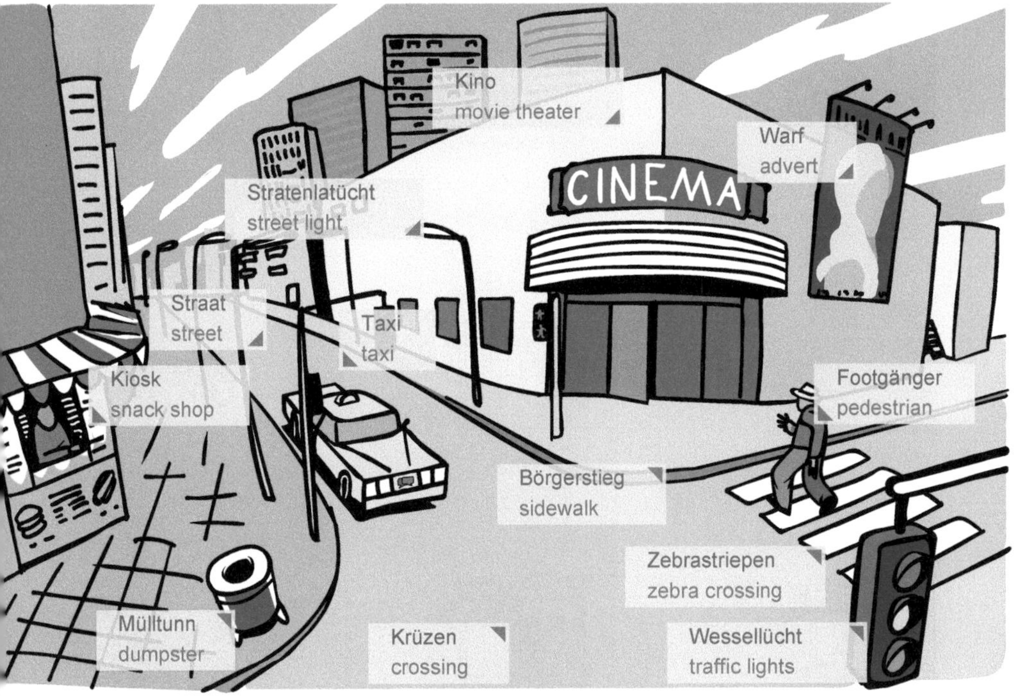

Kino
movie theater

Warf
advert

Stratenlatücht
street light

CINEMA

Straat
street

Taxi
taxi

Footgänger
pedestrian

Kiosk
snack shop

Börgerstieg
sidewalk

Zebrastriepen
zebra crossing

Mülltunn
dumpster

Krüzen
crossing

Wessellücht
traffic lights

Hütt

hut

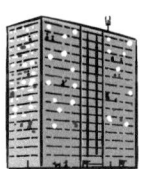

Wahnung

apartment

Bahnhoff

train station

Raathuus

city hall

Museum

museum

School

school

Universität

university

Bank

bank

Krankenhuus

hospital

Hotel

hotel

Afteek

pharmacy

Büro

office

Bookhökerie

book shop

Hökerie

shop

Blomenhökerie

flower shop

Supermarkt

supermarket

Markt

market

Koophuus

department store

Fischhökerie

fishmonger's shop

Inkoopszentrum

mall

Haven

harbor

Parkanlaag

park

Bank

bench

Brüch

bridge

Trepp

stairs

Ünnergrundbahn

subway

Tunnel

tunnel

Busstoppsteed

bus stop

Bar

bar

Spieslokal

restaurant

Breefkassen

postbox

Stratenschild

street sign

Parkklock

parking meter

Deertenpark

zoo

Baadanstalt

swimming pool

Moschee

mosque

Buernhoff

farm

Ümweltversmudden

pollution

Karkhoff

cemetery

Kark

church

Speelplatz

playground

Tempel

temple

Landschop
landscape

Blatt
leaf

Wiespahl
signpost

Weg
path

Wisch
meadow

Steen
stone

Boom
tree

Wannerer
hiker

Fluss
river

Gras
grass

Bloom
flower

Daal
valley

Barg
hill

See
lake

Holt
forest

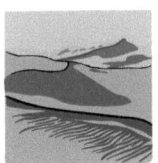
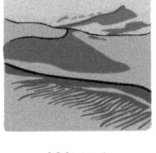

Wööst
desert

Füerspien Barg
volcano

Slott
castle

Regenbagen
rainbow

Poggenstohl
mushroom

Palm
palm tree

Steekmück
mosquito

Fleeg
fly

Miegeemk
ant

Imm
bee

Spinn
spider

Sebber

beetle

Pogg

frog

Katteker

squirrel

Swienegel

hedgehog

Haas

hare

Uul

owl

Vagel

bird

Swaan

swan

Wildswien

boar

Hirsch

deer

Elk

moose

Staudamm

dam

Windrad

wind turbine

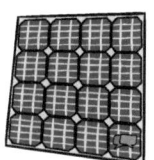

Solarmodul

solar panel

Klima

climate

Kellner
waiter

Spieskoort
menu

Stohl
chair

Supp
soup

Pizza
pizza

Dischdeek
tablecloth

Bestick
cutlery

Vörspies

starter

Haupteten

main course

Nadisch

dessert

Drünk

drinks

Eten

food

Buddel

bottle

Fastfood

fast food

Strateneten

street food

Teekann

teapot

Zuckerdoos

sugar bowl

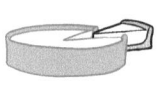

Portschoon

portion

Espressomaschien

espresso machine

Hoochstohl

high chair

Reken

bill

Tablett

tray

Mess

knife

Gavel

fork

Lepel

spoon

Teelepel

teaspoon

Munddook

serviette

Glas

glass

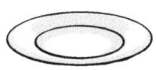

Töller

plate

Suppentöller

soup plate

Ünnertass

saucer

Sooß

sauce

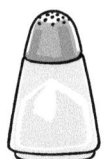

Soltstreuer

salt shaker

Pepermöhl

pepper mill

Etig

vinegar

Ööl

oil

Krüder

spices

Ketchup

ketchup

Mostrich

mustard

Mayonnaise

mayonnaise

Supermarkt
supermarket

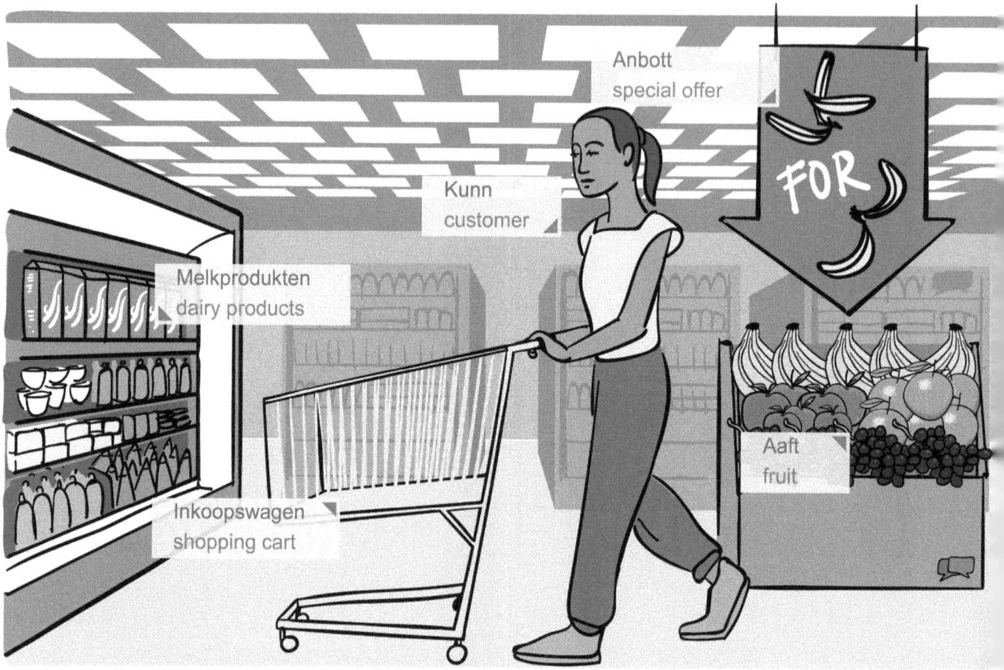

Anbott
special offer

Kunn
customer

Melkprodukten
dairy products

Aaft
fruit

Inkoopswagen
shopping cart

Slachterie	Bäckerie	wegen
butcher's shop	bakery	weigh
	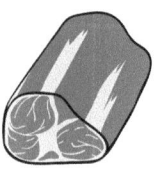	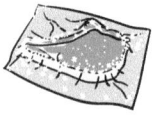
Gröönsaken	Fleesch	Deepköhlkost
vegetables	meat	frozen food

Opsnitt

cold cuts

Konserven

canned food

Waschmiddel

detergent

Snoopkraam

candy

Huushooltssaken

household products

Reinmaaktüüch

cleaning products

Verköpersche

sales representative

Kass

cash register

Kasserer

cashier

Inkoopslist

shopping list

Opsparrtieden

opening hours

Breeftasch

wallet

Kreditkoort

credit card

Tasch

bag

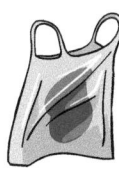

Plastiktüüt

plastic bag

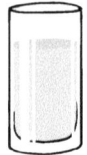

Water

water

Saft

juice

Melk

milk

Cola

coke

Wien

wine

Beer

beer

Spriet

alcohol

Kakao

cocoa

Tee

tea

Koffie

coffee

Espresso

espresso

Cappucino

cappuccino

Banaan

banana

Appel

apple

Appelsien

orange

Meloon

melon

Zitroon

lemon

Wöttel

carrot

Knuuvlook

garlic

Bambus

bamboo

Zibbel

onion

Poggenstohl

mushroom

Nööt

nuts

Nudeln

noodles

Spaghetti

spaghetti

Ries

rice

Salat

salad

Pommes frites

fries

Braadkantüffeln

fried potatoes

Pizza

pizza

Hamborger

hamburger

Sandwich

sandwich

Snitzel

escalope

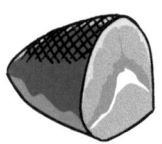

Schinken

ham

Salami

salami

Wust

sausage

Hohn

chicken

Braden

roast

Fisch

fish

Eten - food

Haverflocken

porridge oats

Müsli

muesli

Cornflakes

cornflakes

Mehl

flour

Croissant

croissant

Rundstück

bread roll

Broot

bread

Toast

toast

Keksen

cookies

Botter

butter

Quark

curd

Koken

cake

Ei

egg

Spegelei

fried egg

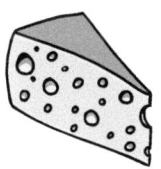

Kees

cheese

Ies

ice cream

Zucker

sugar

Honnig

honey

Marmelaad

jelly

Nougat-Creme

nougat cream

Curry

curry

Buernhoff
farm

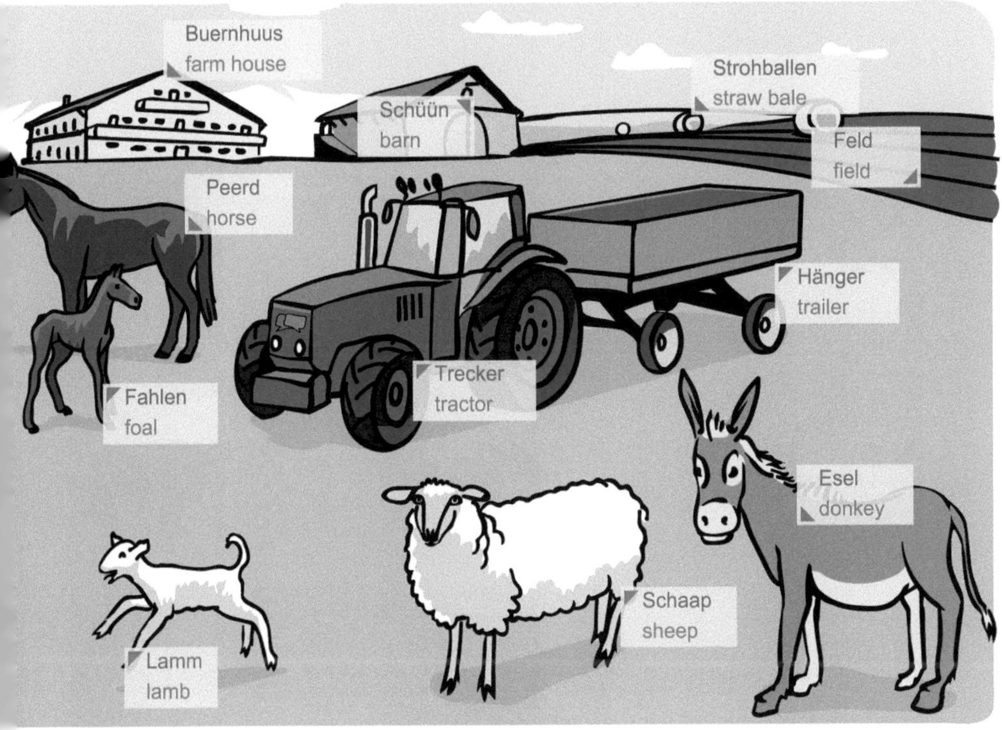
Buernhuus
farm house
Schüün
barn
Strohballen
straw bale
Feld
field
Peerd
horse
Hänger
trailer
Trecker
tractor
Fahlen
foal
Esel
donkey
Schaap
sheep
Lamm
lamb

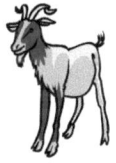

Zeeg
goat

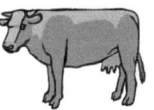

Koh
cow

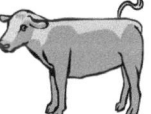

Kalf
calf

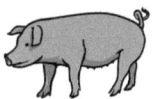

Swien
pig

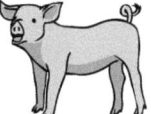

Farken
piglet

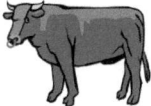

Bull
bull

Goos

goose

Aant

duck

Küken

chick

Hohn

hen

Hahn

cockerel

Rott

rat

Katt

cat

Muus

mouse

Oss

ox

Hund

dog

Hunnenhütt

dog house

Goornslauch

garden hose

Geetkann

watering can

Lee

scythe

Ploog

plow

Sich

sickle

Hack

hoe

Mestfork

pitchfork

Ext

axe

Schuufkoor

pushcart

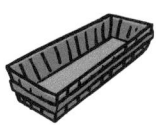

Trog

trough

Melkkann

milk can

Sack

sack

Tuun

fence

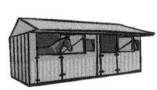

Stall

stable

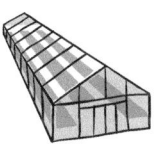

Drievhuus

greenhouse

Bodden

soil

Saat

seed

Dünger

fertilizer

Meihdöscher

combine harvester

oornen

harvest

Oorn

harvest

Yamswöttel

yams

Weten

wheat

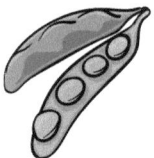

Soja

soya

Kantüffel

potato

Törksche Weten

corn

Rapp

rapeseed

Aaftboom

fruit tree

Troopsch Kantüffel

manioc

Koorn

grain

Huus
house

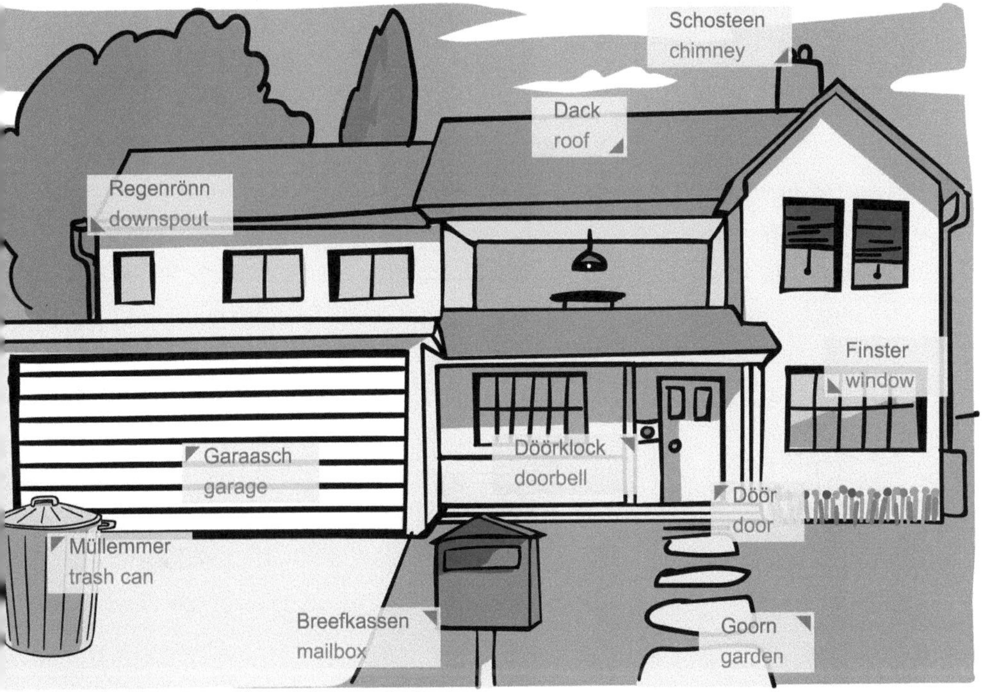
Schosteen
chimney
Dack
roof
Regenrönn
downspout
Finster
window
Döörklock
doorbell
Garaasch
garage
Döör
door
Müllemmer
trash can
Breefkassen
mailbox
Goorn
garden

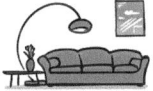

Wahnstuuv

living room

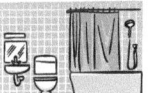

Baadstuuv

bathroom

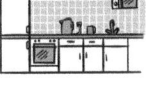

Kööк

kitchen

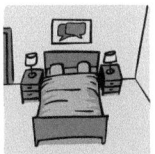

Slaapstuuv

bedroom

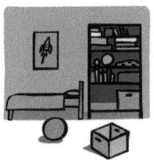

Kinnerstuuv

kids room

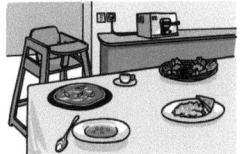

Eetstuuv

dining room

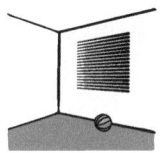

Footbodden
floor

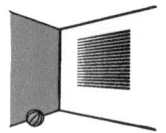

Wand
wall

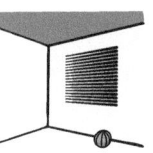

Deek
ceiling

Keller
cellar

Hittluftbad
sauna

Balkon
balcony

Terrass
terrace

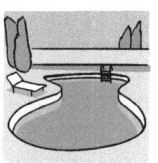

Swümmbad
pool

Rasenmeiher
lawn mower

Bettbetog
sheet

Bettdeek
bedspread

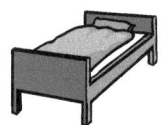

Puuch
bed

Bessen
broom

Emmer
bucket

Schalter
switch

Wahnstuuv
living room

Tapeet
wallpaper
Bild
picture
Lamp
lamp
Regal
shelf
Schapp
cabinet
Kiekkassen
television
Kamin
fireplace
Bloom
flower
Küssen
cushion
Sofa
sofa
Vaas
vase
Feernbedenen
remote control

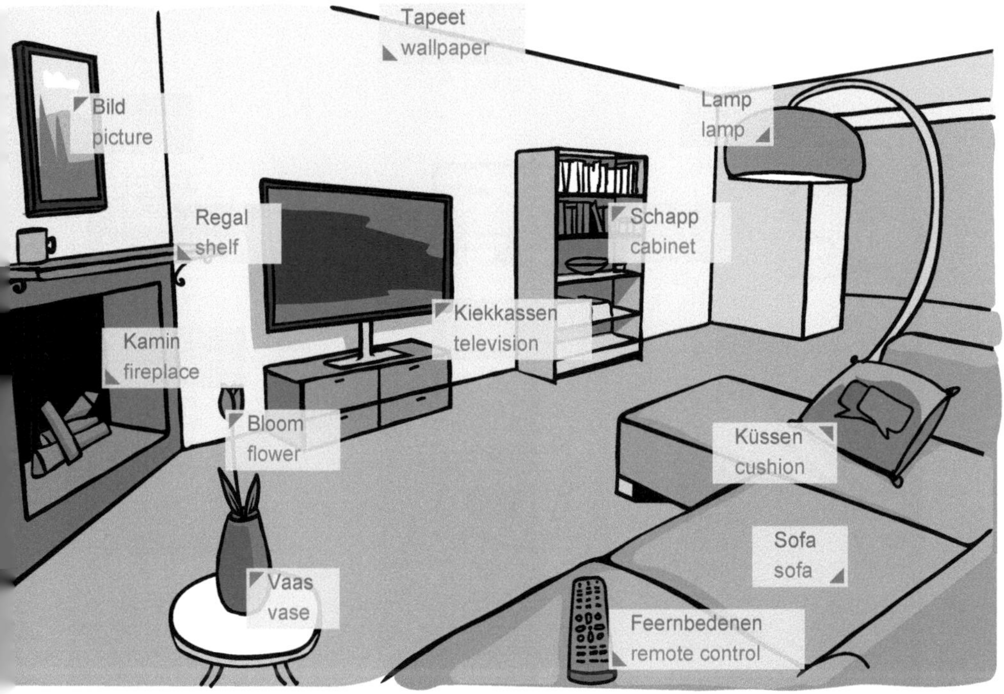

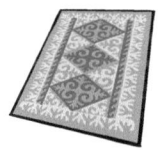

Teppich
carpet

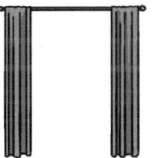

Vörhang
drape

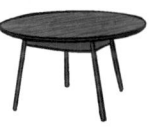

Disch
table

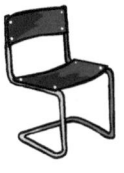

Stohl
chair

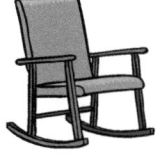

Schuckelstohl
rocking chair

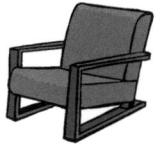

Sessel
armchair

Book	**Deek**	**Dekoratschoon**
book	blanket	decoration

Füerholt	**Film**	**Stereoanlaag**
firewood	film	stereo system

Slötel	**Narichtenblatt**	**Gemälde**
key	newspaper	painting

Poster	**Radio**	**Opschrievblock**
poster	radio	notebook

Huulbessen	**Kaktus**	**Kars**
vacuum cleaner	cactus	candle

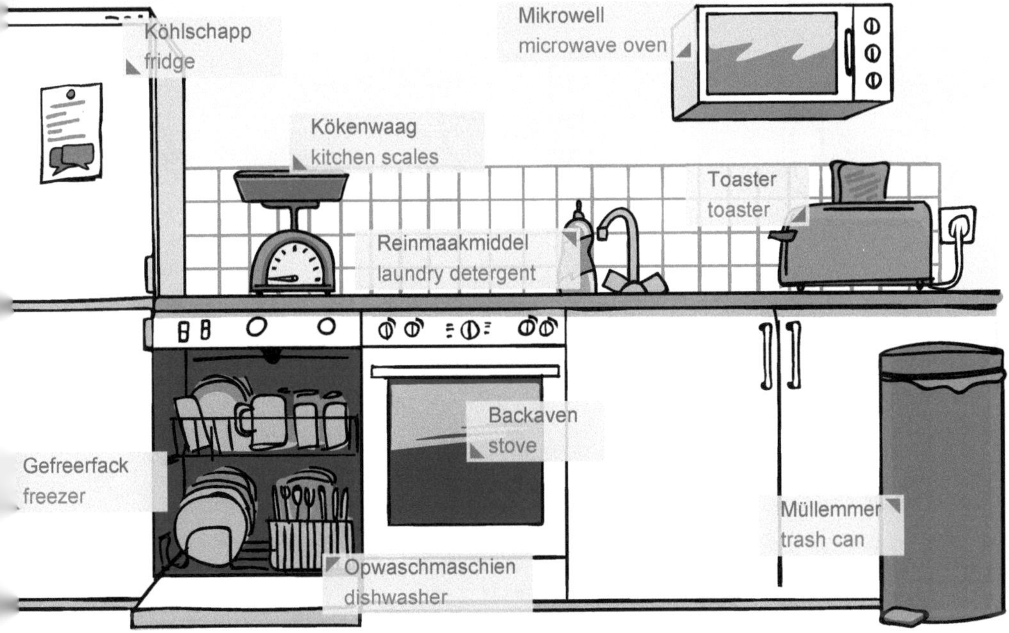

Köhlschapp
fridge

Mikrowell
microwave oven

Kökenwaag
kitchen scales

Toaster
toaster

Reinmaakmiddel
laundry detergent

Backaven
stove

Gefreerfack
freezer

Müllemmer
trash can

Opwaschmaschien
dishwasher

Heerd
cooker

Pott
pot

Gussiesern Putt
cast-iron pot

Wok / Kadai
wok / kadai

Pann
pan

Waterkaker
kettle

Dampkaakputt

steamer

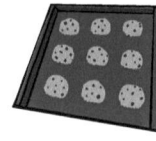

Backblick

baking tray

Geschirr

crockery

Beker

mug

Schaal

bowl

Eetsticken

chopsticks

Suppenkell

ladle

Pannenwenner

spatula

Sneebessen

whisk

Kaakseef

strainer

Seef

sieve

Riev

grater

Mörser

mortar

Grill

barbecue

Füerstell

fireplace

Sniedbrett

chopping board

Nudelholt

rolling pin

Proppentrecker

corkscrew

Doos

can

Dosenaapner

can opener

Pottlappen

oven cloth

Waschbecken

sink

Böst

brush

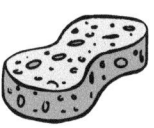

Swamm

sponge

Mixer

blender

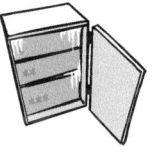

Iesschapp

deep freezer

Nuckelbuddel

baby bottle

Waterhahn

tap

Köök - kitchen

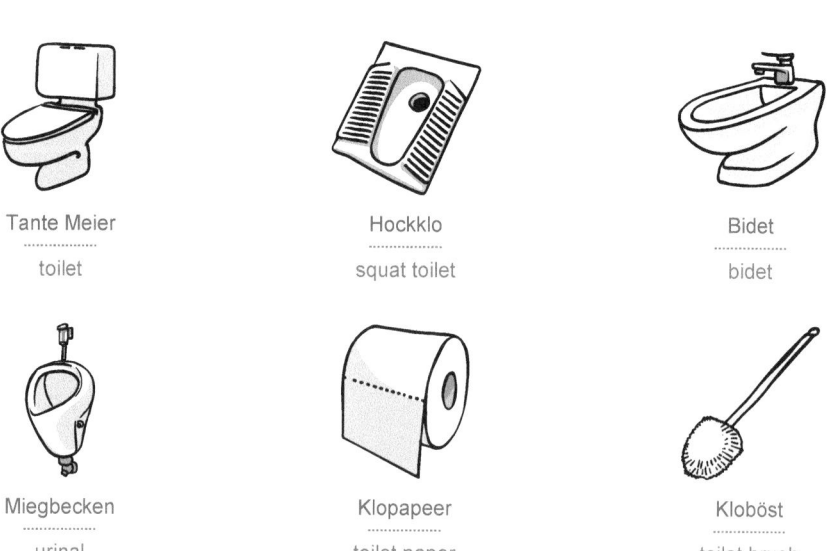

Baadstuuv

bathroom

Bruus
shower
Heizung
heating
Handdook
towel
Bruusvörhang
shower curtain
Schuumbad
bubble bath
Baadwann
bathtub
Glas
glass
Waschmaschien
washing machine
Waterhahn
tap
Fliesen
tiles
lütte Putt
potty
Waschbecken
sink

Tante Meier

toilet

Hockklo

squat toilet

Bidet

bidet

Miegbecken

urinal

Klopapeer

toilet paper

Kloböst

toilet brush

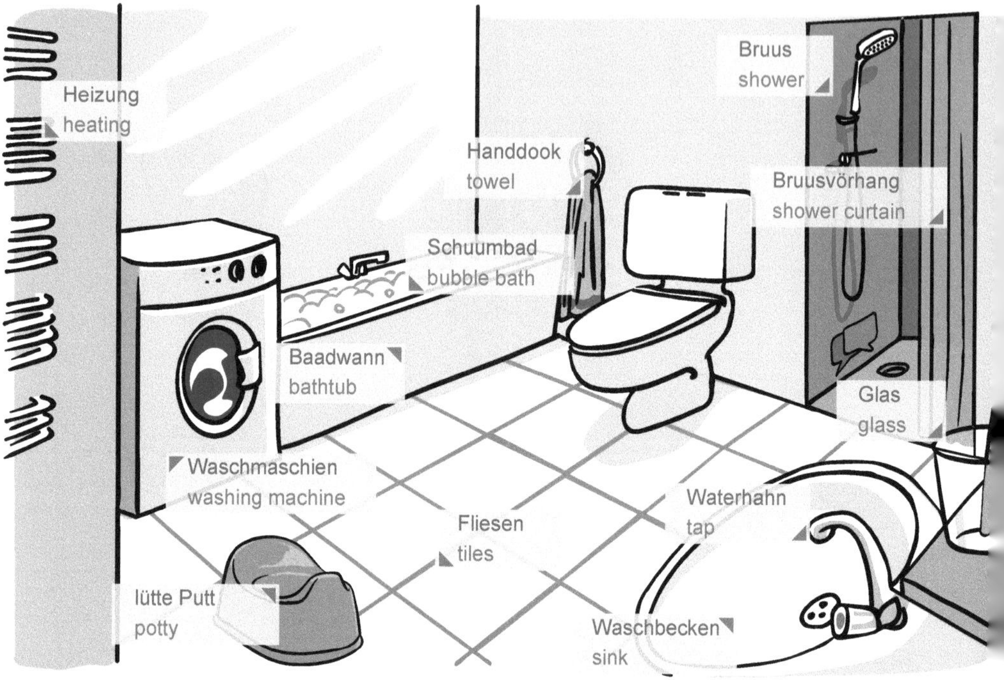

Tähnböst

toothbrush

Tähnpast

toothpaste

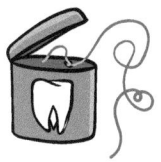

Tähnsied

dental floss

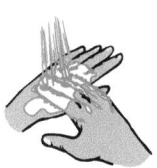

waschen

wash

Handbruus

hand shower

Intimbruus

douche

Waschschöttel

basin

Rüchböst

back brush

Seep

soap

Bruusgeel

shower gel

Hoorwaschmiddel

shampoo

Waschlappen

flannel

Afloop

drain

Creme

creme

Deodorant

deodorant

Baadstuuv - bathroom

Spegel

mirror

Kosmetikspegel

hand mirror

Raserer

razor

Raseerschuum

shaving foam

Raseerwater

aftershave

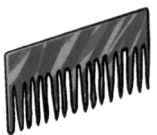

Kamm

comb

Böst

brush

Hoordröger

hair-dryer

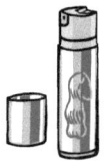

Hoorspray

hairspray

Smink

makeup

Lippensticken

lipstick

Nagellack

nail varnish

Watt

cotton wool

Nagelscheer

nail scissors

Rüükwater

perfume

Kulturbüdel

washbag

Schemel

stool

Waag

weighing scales

Baadmantel

bathrobe

Gummihanschen

rubber gloves

Tampon

tampon

Damenbinn

sanitary towel

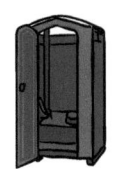

Chemieklo

chemical toilet

Kinnerstuuv

kids room

Wecker
alarm clock
Knudeldeert
cuddly toy
Speeltüüchauto
toy car
Klöter
rattle
Poppenhuus
doll's house
Geschenk
present

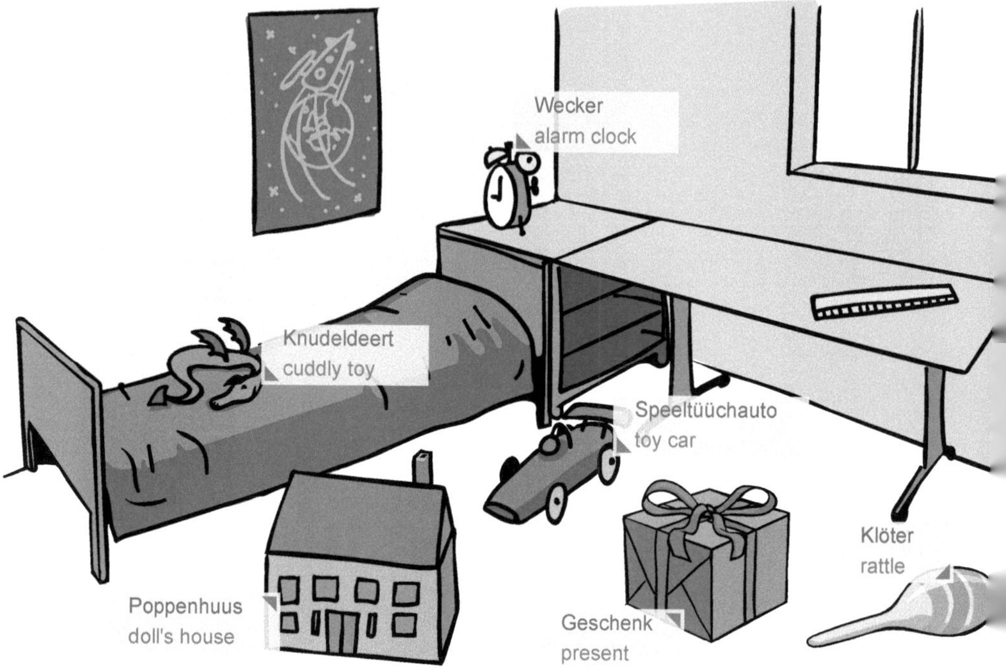

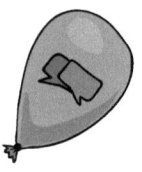

Luftballon

balloon

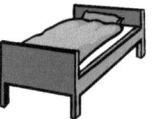

Puuch

bed

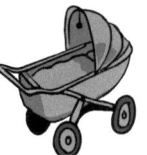

Kinnerwagen

stroller

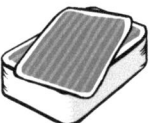

Koortenspeel

deck of cards

Puzzle

jigsaw

SUPER
MEGA

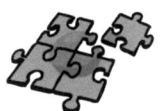

Billergeschicht

comic

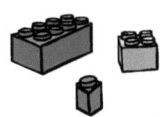

Legostenen

lego bricks

Bustenen

toy blocks

Action-Figur

action figure

Strampelantog

romper suit

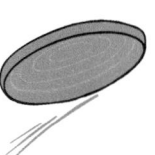

Frisbeeschiev

frisbee

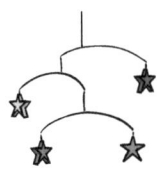

Mobile

mobile

Brettspeel

board game

Wörpel

dice

Modelliesenbahn

model train set

Snuller

pacifier

Party

party

Billerbook

picture book

Ball

ball

Popp

doll

spelen

play

Sandkassen

sandpit

Schuckel

swing

Speeltüüch

toys

Speelkonsool

video game console

Dreerad

tricycle

Teddyboor

teddy bear

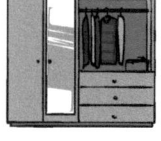

Klederschapp

wardrobe

Tüüch

clothing

Socken

socks

Strümp

stockings

Strumpbüx

tights

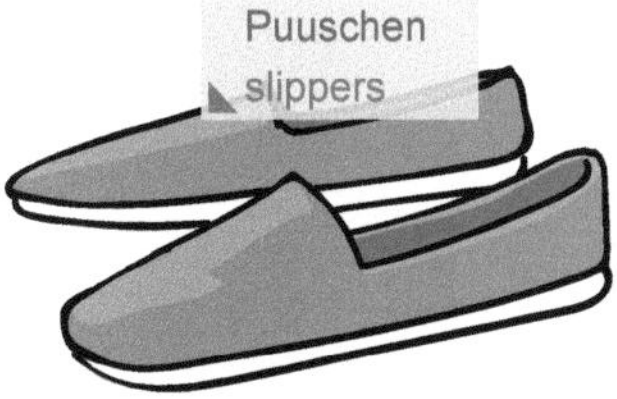

Halsdook
scarf

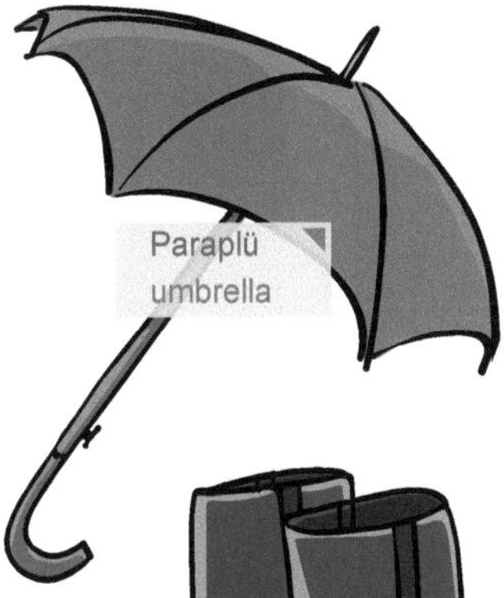

Paraplü
umbrella

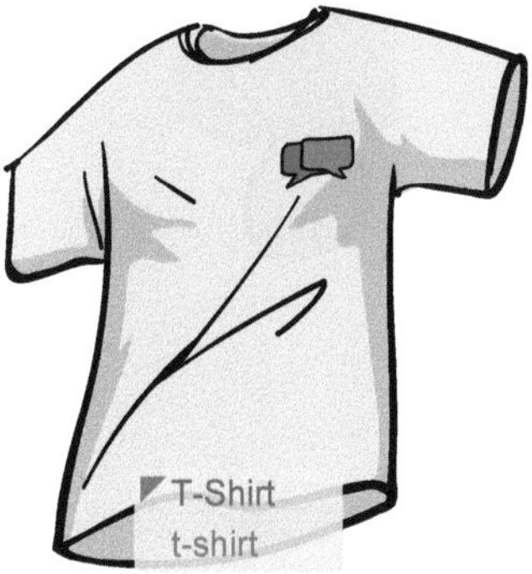

T-Shirt
t-shirt

Liefreem
belt

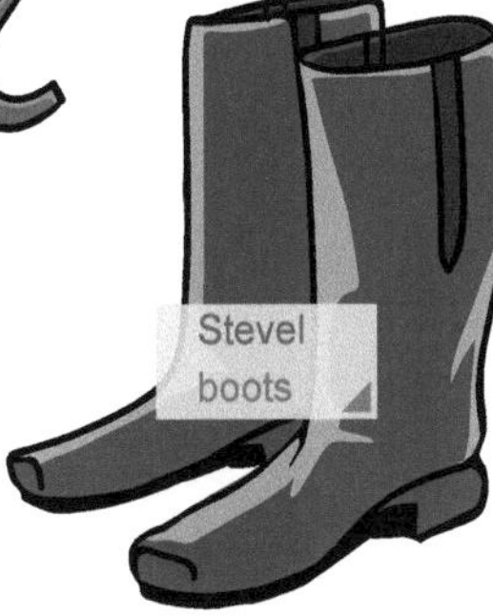

Stevel
boots

Puuschen
slippers

Turnschoh
sneakers

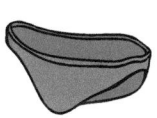

Sandalen
·············
sandals

Schoh
·············
shoes

Gummistevel
·············
rubber boots

Ünnerbüx
·············
underwear

Bostholler
·············
bra

Ünnerhemd
·············
undershirt

Tüüch - clothing   45

Lief

body

Büx

pants

Jeansnüx

jeans

Rock

skirt

Bluus

blouse

Hemd

shirt

Pullover

pullover

Kapuzenpullover

sweater

Blazer

blazer

Jack

jacket

Mantel

coat

Övertrecker

raincoat

Kostüm

costume

Kleed

dress

Hochtietskleed

wedding dress

Antog

suit

Nachtkleed

nightgown

Slaapantog

pajamas

Sari

sari

Koppdook

headscarf

Turban

turban

Burka

burka

Kaftan

kaftan

Abaya

abaya

Baadantog

swimsuit

Baadbüx

trunks

Korte Büx

shorts

Antog to'n Öven

tracksuit

Schört

apron

Handschoh

gloves

Knopp

button

Brill

glasses

Armband

bracelet

Halskeed

necklace

Ring

ring

Ohrbummel

earring

Mütz

cap

Klederbögel

coat hanger

Hoot

hat

Binner

tie

Rietslüter

zip

Helm

helmet

Drachtband

braces

Schooluniform

school uniform

Uniform

uniform

Severböten

bib

Snuller

pacifier

Winnel

diaper

Büro
office

Server
server

Aktenschapp
filing cabinet

Drucker
printer

Papeer
paper

Bildschirm
monitor

Schrievdisch
desk

Muus
mouse

Orner
folder

Knoopboord
keyboard

Papeerkorf
waste-paper basket

Computer
computer

Stohl
chair

Koffiebeker

coffee mug

Taschenreekner

calculator

Internet

internet

Klappreekner

laptop

Breef

letter

Naricht

message

Ackersnacker

cell phone

Nettwark

network

Kopeerapparat

photocopier

Software

software

Klöönkassen

telephone

Steekdoos

plug socket

Faxapparat

fax machine

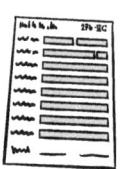

Formulor

form

Dokument

document

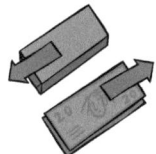

köpen

buy

betahlen

pay

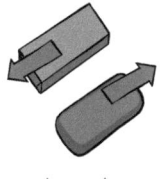

hanneln

trade

Geld

money

 **USD**

Dollar

dollar

 **EUR**

Euro

euro

 **JPY**

Yen

yen

 **RUB**

Ruvel

rouble

 **CHF**

Swiezer Franken

Swiss franc

 **CNY**

Renminbi Yuan

renminbi yuan

 **INR**

Rupie

rupee

Geldautomat

cash point

Wesselstuuv

currency exchange office

Gold

gold

Sülver

silver

Ööl

oil

Energie

energy

Pries

price

Verdrag

contract

Stüer

tax

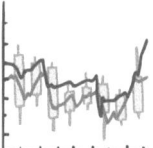

Andeelschien

stock

arbeiden

work

Anstellte

employee

Arbeitgever

employer

Fabrik

factory

Hökerie

shop

Profeschonen
occupations

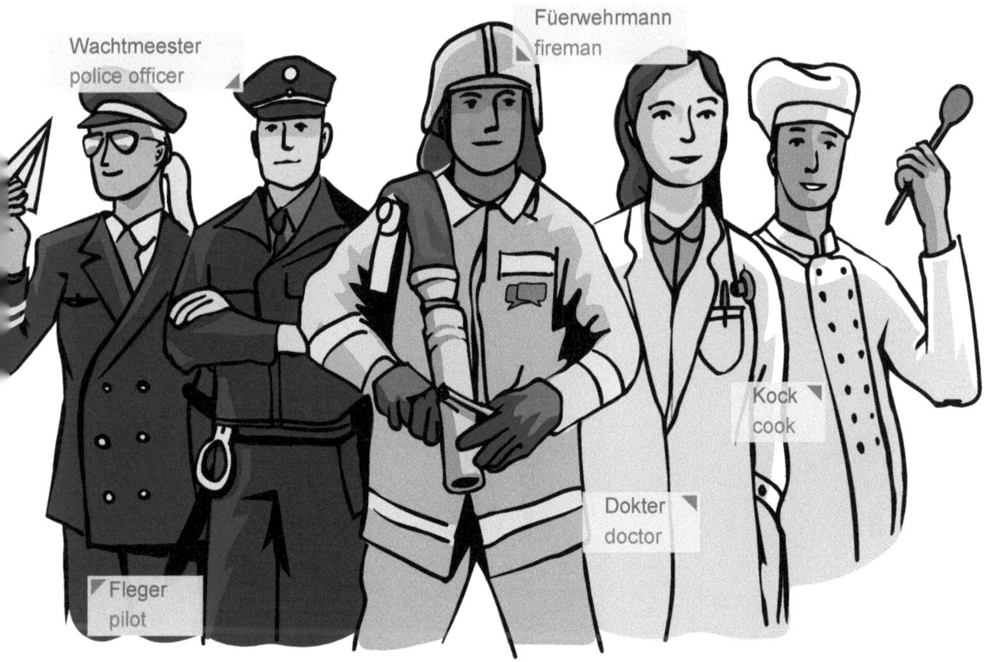
Wachtmeester
police officer
Füerwehrmann
fireman
Kock
cook
Dokter
doctor
Fleger
pilot

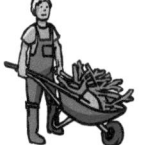

Goorner

gardener

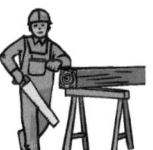

Discher

carpenter

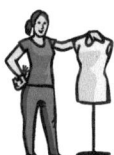

Neihersche

seamstress

Richter

judge

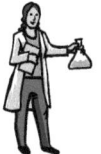

Chemiker

chemist

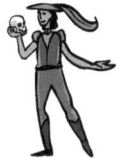

Schauspeler

actor

Busfohrer

bus driver

Taxifohrer

taxi driver

Fischer

fisherman

Reinmaakfru

cleaning lady

Dackdecker

roofer

Kellner

waiter

Jäger

hunter

Maler

painter

Bäcker

baker

Elektriker

electrician

Buarbeider

builder

Ingenieur

engineer

Slachter

butcher

Klempner

plumber

Postbüdel

postman

Suldat

soldier

Architekt

architect

Kasserer

cashier

Florist

florist

Putzbüdel

hairdresser

Schaffner

conductor

Mechaniker

mechanic

Kaptein

captain

Tähndokter

dentist

Wetenschopler

scientist

Rabbi

rabbi

Imam

imam

Mönk

monk

Paap

pastor

Warktüüch

tools

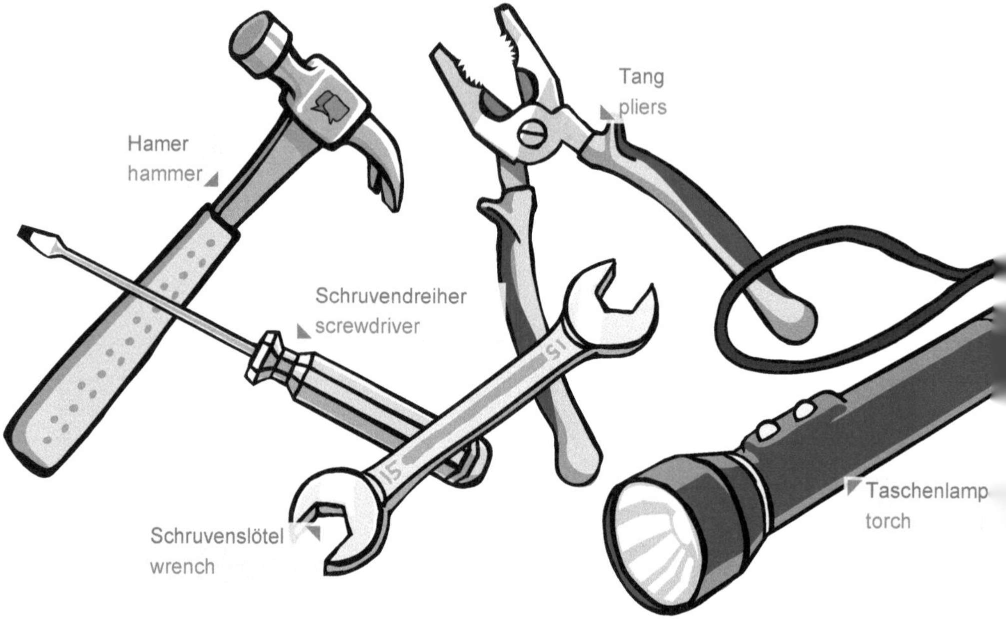
Hamer
hammer
Tang
pliers
Schruvendreiher
screwdriver
Schruvenslötel
wrench
Taschenlamp
torch

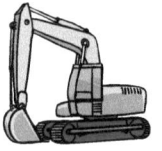

Grieper
excavator

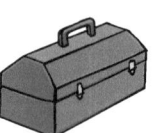

Warktüüchkassen
toolbox

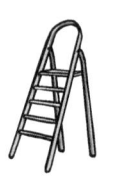

Ledder
ladder

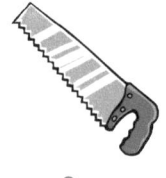

Saag
saw

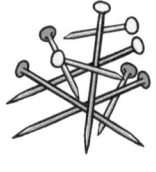

Nagels
nails

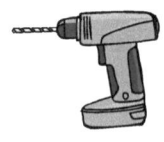

Bohrer
drill

heelmaken
repair

Schüffel
shovel

Schiet!
Damn!

Kehrblick
dustpan

Farvpott
paint can

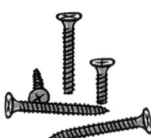

Schruven
screws

Musikinstrumenten
musical instruments

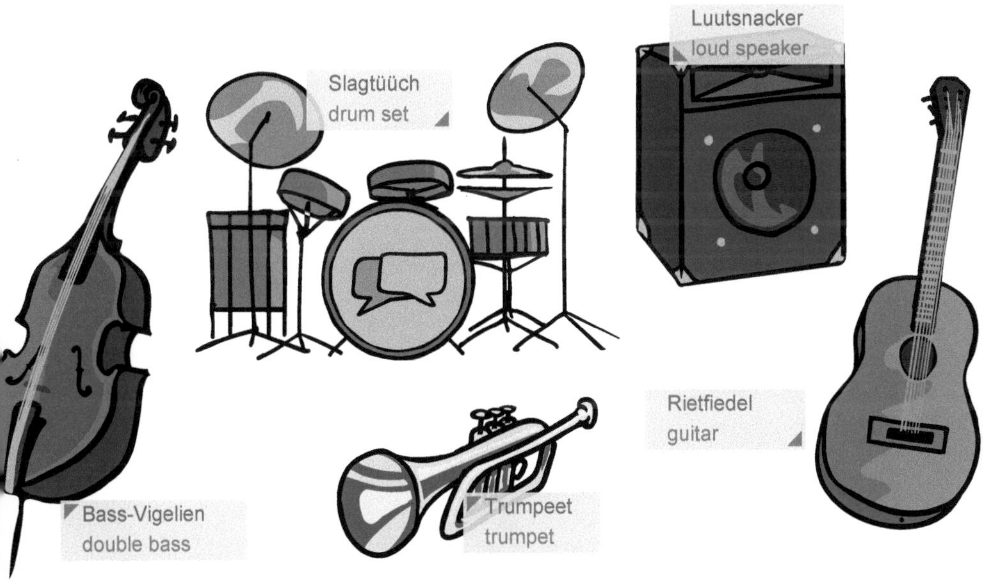

Luutsnacker
loud speaker

Slagtüüch
drum set

Rietfiedel
guitar

Bass-Vigelien
double bass

Trumpeet
trumpet

Klaveer

piano

Vigelien

violin

Bass

bass

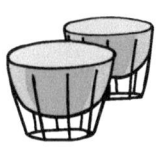

Pauk

timpani

Trummeln

drums

Keyboard

keyboard

Saxophon

saxophone

Fleut

flute

Mikrofoon

microphone

Deertenpark

zoo

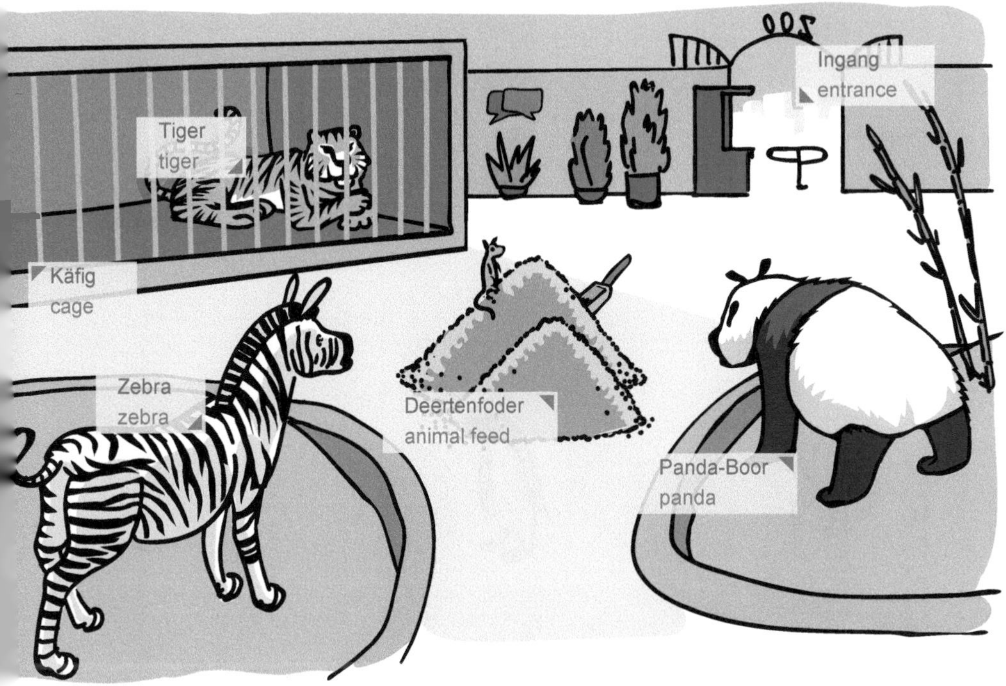

Ingang
entrance
Tiger
tiger
Käfig
cage
Zebra
zebra
Deertenfoder
animal feed
Panda-Boor
panda

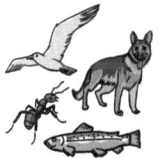

Deerten

animals

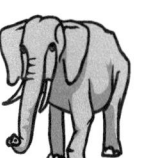

Elefant

elephant

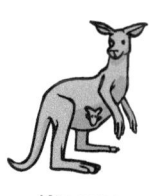

Känguru

kangaroo

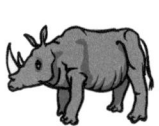

Neeshoorn

rhino

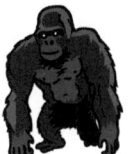

Gorilla

gorilla

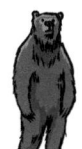

Boor

bear

Kameel

camel

Struuß

ostrich

Lööv

lion

Aap

monkey

Flamingo

flamingo

Papagoi

parrot

Iesboor

polar bear

Pinguin

penguin

Haifisch

shark

Pageluun

peacock

Slang

snake

Krokodil

crocodile

Oppasser in'n Deertenpark

zookeeper

Saalhund

seal

Jaguor

jaguar

Pony

pony

Leopard

leopard

Nilpeerd

hippo

Giraff

giraffe

Aadler

eagle

Wildswien

boar

Fisch

fish

Schildkrööt

turtle

Walross

walrus

Voss

fox

Gazell

gazelle

Amerikaansch Football
American football

Radfohren
cycling

Tennis
tennis

Korfball
basketball

Swümmen
swimming

Boxen
boxing

Ieshockey
ice hockey

Football
soccer

Fedderball
badminton

Leichtathletik
athletics

Handball
handball

Skilopen
skiing

Polo
polo

springen
jump

lachen
laugh

ümarmen
hug

gahn
walk

singen
sing

drömen
dream

beden
pray

snuteln
kiss

schrieven
....
write

teken
....
draw

wiesen
....
show

drücken
....
push

geven
....
give

nehmen
....
take

hebben

have

doon

do

sien

be

stahn

stand

lopen

run

trecken

pull

smieten

throw

fallen

fall

liggen

lie

töven

wait

dregen

carry

sitten

sit

antrecken

get dressed

slapen

sleep

opwaken

wake up

ankieken

look at

wenen

cry

eien

stroke

kämmen

comb

snacken

talk

verstahn

understand

fragen

ask

hören

listen

drinken

drink

eten

eat

oprümen

tidy up

leefhebben

love

kaken

cook

fohren

drive

flegen

fly

Aktivitäten - activities

65

segeln

sail

reken

calculate

lesen

read

lehren

learn

arbeiden

work

de Plünnen tohoopsmieten

marry

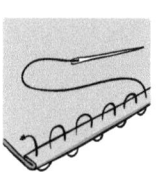

neihen

sew

Tähnen putzen

brush teeth

dootmaken

kill

smöken

smoke

schicken

send

Grootmoder
grandmother

Grootvadder
grandfather

Vadder
father

Moder
mother

Winnelkind
baby

Dochter
daughter

Söhn
son

Gast

guest

Tant

aunt

Unkel

uncle

Broder

brother

Süster

sister

Lief

body

Vörkopp
forehead
Oog
eye
Schuller
shoulder
Finger
finger
Gesicht
face
Kinn
chin
Hand
hand
Been
leg
Bost
breast
Arm
arm

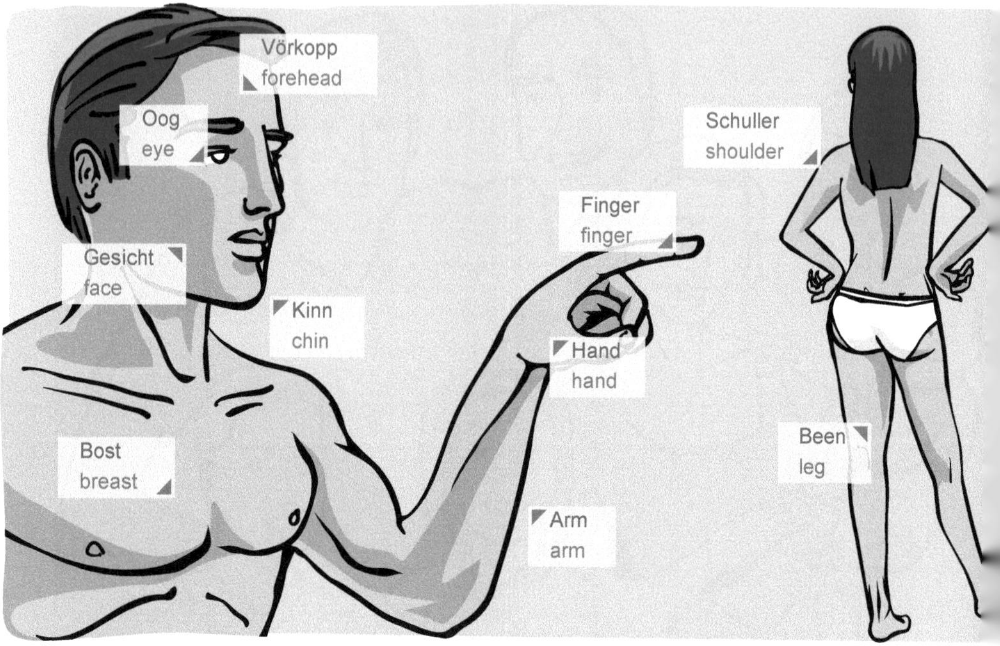

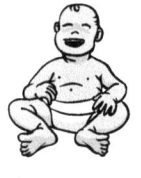

Winnelkind

baby

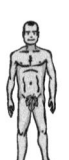

Mann

man

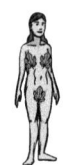

Fro

woman

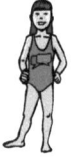

Deern

girl

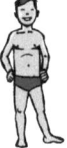

Jung

boy

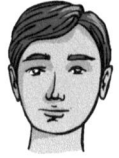

Arm

head

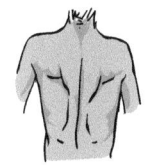

Rüch

back

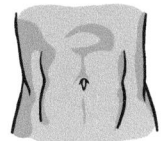

Buuk

belly

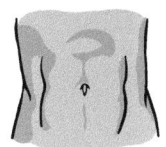

Navel

navel

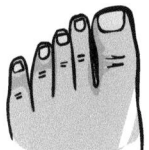

Teh

toe

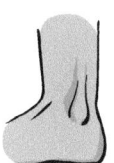

Hack

heel

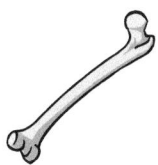

Knaken

bone

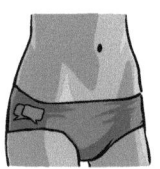

Hüft

hip

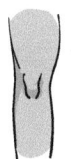

Knee

knee

Ellbagen

elbow

Nees

nose

Achtersen

buttocks

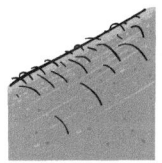

Huut

skin

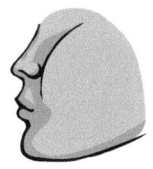

Back

cheek

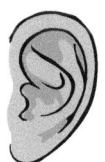

Ohr

ear

Lipp

lip

Lief - body 69

Mund

mouth

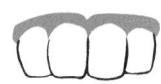

Tähn

tooth

Tung

tongue

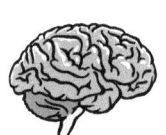

Bregen

brain

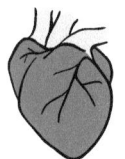

Hart

heart

Muskel

muscle

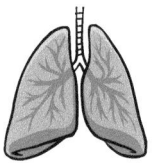

Lung

lung

Lever

liver

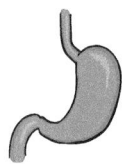

Maag

stomach

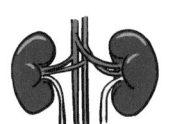

Neren

kidneys

Bislaap

sex

Kondoom

condom

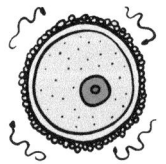

Eizell

ovum

Sperma

semen

Anner Ümstänn

pregnancy

Lief - body

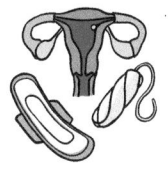

Menstruatschoon

menstruation

Scheed

vagina

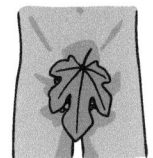

Pint

penis

Ogenbroe

eyebrow

Hoor

hair

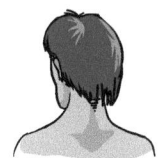

Hals

neck

Krankenhuus
hospital

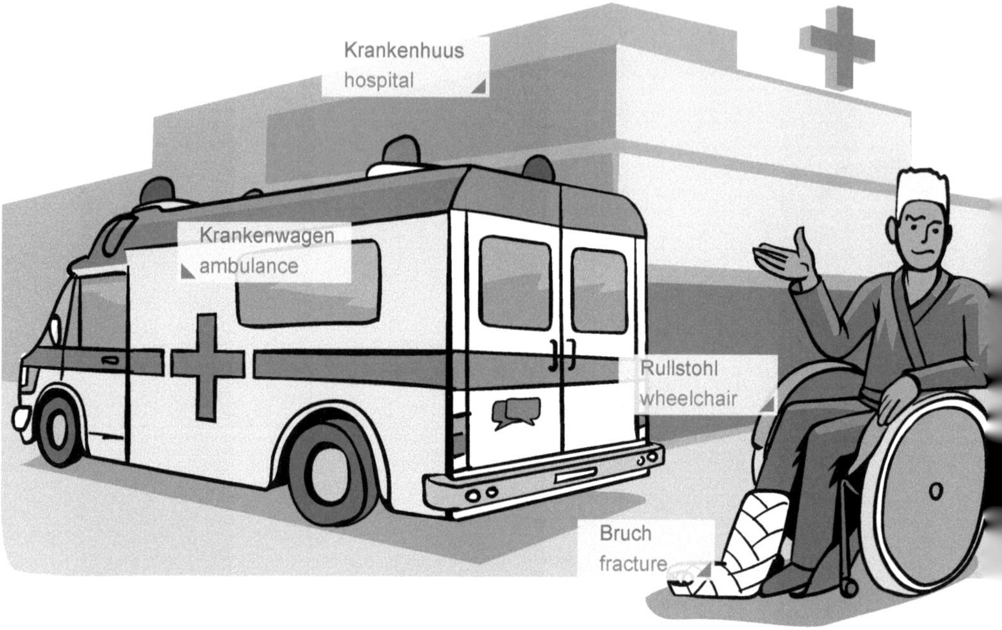

Krankenhuus
hospital
Krankenwagen
ambulance
Rullstohl
wheelchair
Bruch
fracture

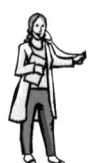

Dokter

doctor

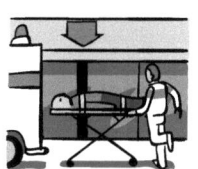

Nootopnahm

emergency room

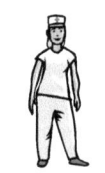

Krankensüster

nurse

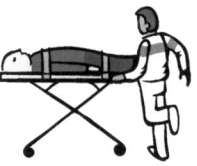

Nootfall

emergency

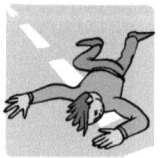

ahnmächtig

unconscious

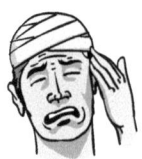

Wehdaag

pain

Verwunnen

injury

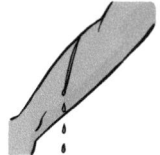

Blöden

bleeding

Hartinfarkt

heart attack

Slaganfall

stroke

Allergie

allergy

Hoosten

cough

Fever

fever

Gripp

flu

Dörchfall

diarrhea

Koppwehdaag

headache

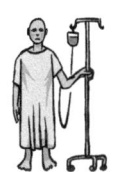

Kreeft

cancer

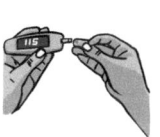

Zuckersüük

diabetes

Chirurg

surgeon

Chirurgsch Mess

scalpel

Operatschoon

operation

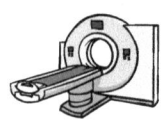

CT

CT

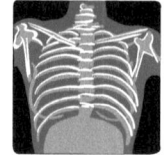

Dörchlüchten

x-ray

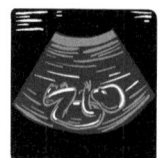

Ultraschall

ultrasound

Mask

face mask

Krankheit

disease

Töövruum

waiting room

Krück

crutch

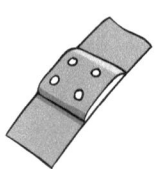

Plaaster

plaster

Verband

bandage

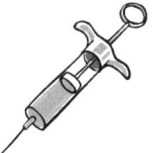

Insprütten

injection

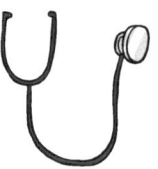

Stethoskop

stethoscope

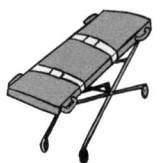

Draag

stretcher

Feverthermometer

clinical thermometer

Geboort

birth

Övergewicht

overweight

Höörapparat

hearing aid

Kiemfriemiddel

disinfectant

Ansteken

infection

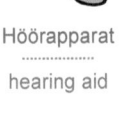

Virus

virus

HIV / AIDS

HIV / AIDS

Heelmiddel

medicine

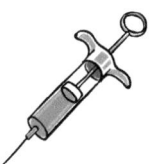

Impen

vaccination

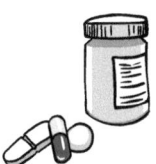

Tabletten

tablets

Pill

pill

Nootroop

emergency call

Blootdruck-Meter

blood pressure monitor

krank / gesund

ill / healthy

Hölp!	Alarm	Överfall
Help!	alarm	assault
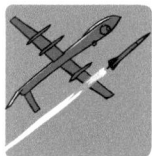		
Angreep	Gefohr	Nootutgang
attack	danger	emergency exit

Füer!	Füerlöscher	Unfall
Fire!	fire extinguisher	accident
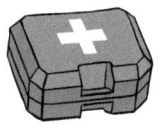		
Noothölpkoffer	SOS	Polizei
first-aid kit	SOS	police

Europa

Europe

Noordamerika

North America

Süüdamerika

South America

Afrika

Africa

Asien

Asia

Australien

Australia

Atlantik

Atlantic

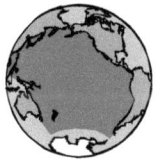

Pazifik

Pacific

Indisch Weltmeer

Indian Ocean

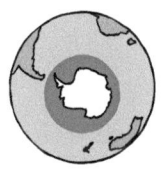

ntarktisch Weltmeer

Antarctic Ocean

Arktisch Weltmeer

Arctic Ocean

Noordpol

North pole

Süüdpol

South pole

Antarktis

Antarctica

Eerd

earth

Land

land

See

sea

Eiland

island

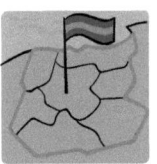

Natschoon

nation

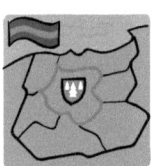

Staat

state

Tallenblatt

clock face

Stunnenwieser

hour hand

Minutenwieser

minute hand

Sekunnenwieser

second hand

Wo laat is dat?

What time is it?

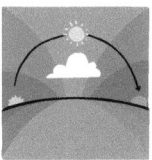

Dag

day

Tiet

time

nu

now

digetaalsch Klock

digital watch

Minuut

minute

Stunn

hour

Week

week

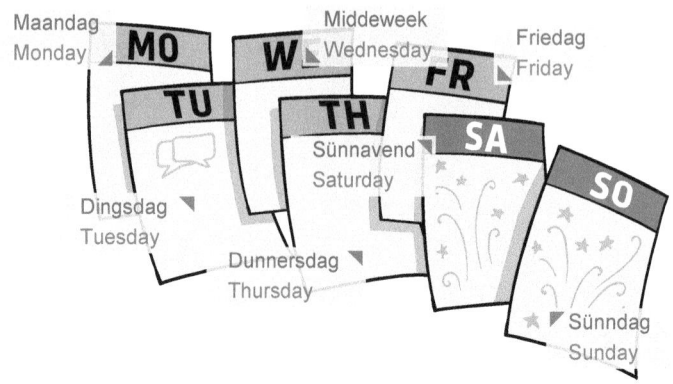

Maandag / Monday
Middeweek / Wednesday
Friedag / Friday
Dingsdag / Tuesday
Dunnersdag / Thursday
Sünnavend / Saturday
Sünndag / Sunday

güstern
....
yesterday

hüüt
....
today

morgen
....
tomorrow

Morgen
....
morning

Meddag
....
noon

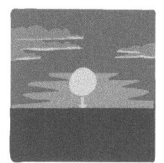

Avend
....
evening

Arbeitsdaag
....
workdays

Wekenenn
....
weekend

Johr

year

Regen
rain
Regenbagen
rainbow
Wind
wind
Snee
snow
Fröhjohr
spring
Harvst
fall
Sommer
summer
Winter
winter

4.APRIL 11°
5.APRIL 4°
6.APRIL 13°
7.APRIL 8°
8.APRIL 10°

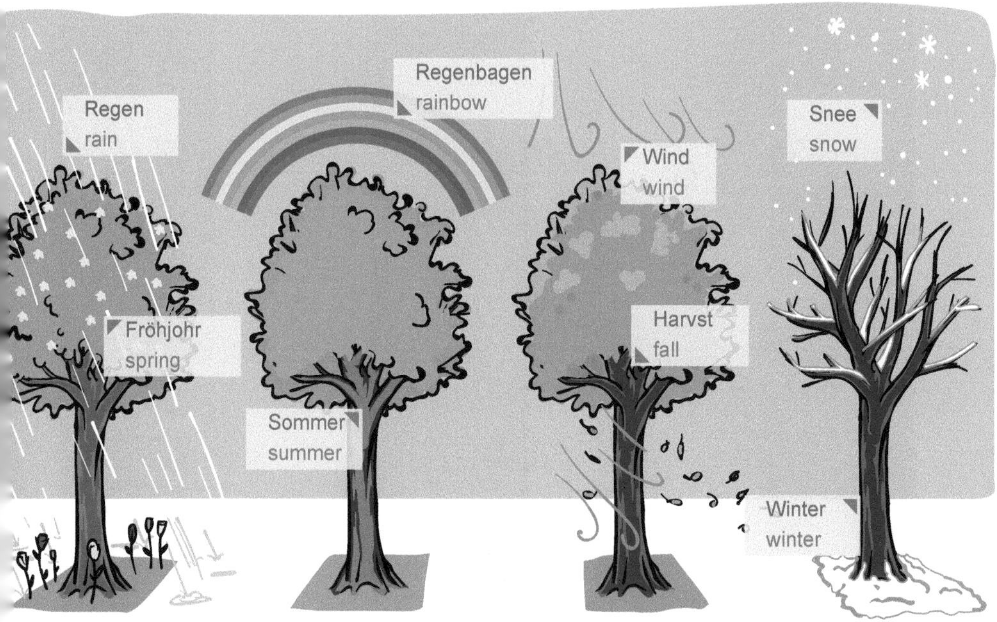

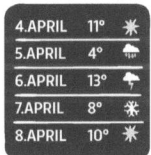

Wedervörhersaag
weather forecast

F C
120 40
90 30
60 20
30 10
0 0
-30 -10
-20

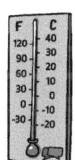

Thermometer
thermometer

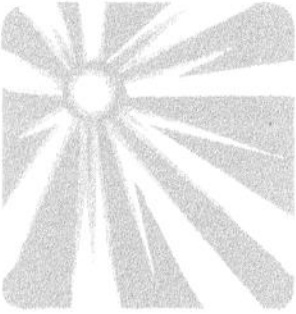

Sünnenschien
sunshine

Wulk
cloud

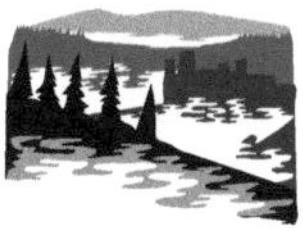

Nevel
fog

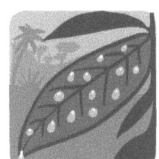

Luftfuchtigkeit
humidity

Blitz

lightning

Dunner

thunder

Storm

storm

Hagel

hail

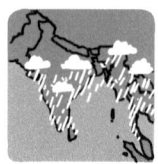

Monsun

monsoon

Floot

flood

les

ice

Januormaand

January

Februormaand

February

Martmaand

March

Aprilmaand

April

Maimaand

May

Junimaand

June

Julimaand

July

Augustmaand

August

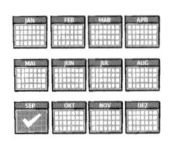

Septembermaand
September

Oktobermaand
October

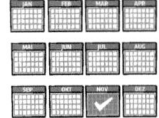

Novembermaand
November

Dezembermaand
December

Formen
shapes

Krink
circle

Quadrat
square

Rechteck
rectangle

Dreeeck
triangle

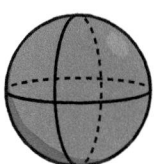

Kugel
sphere

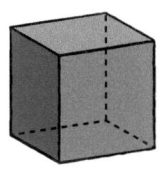

Wörpel
cube

Farven
colors

witt

white

geel

yellow

orangsch

orange

pink

pink

root

red

lila

purple

blau

blue

gröön

green

bruun

brown

gries

gray

swart

black

veel / wenig

a lot / a little

böös / verdreeglich

angry / calm

smuck / mies

beautiful / ugly

Begünn / Enn

beginning / end

groot / lütt

big / small

hell / düüster

bright / dark

Broder / Süster

brother / sister

schier / schietig

clean / dirty

kumpleet / nich kumpleet

complete / incomplete

Dag / Nacht

day / night

doot / lebennig

dead / alive

breet / small

wide / narrow

geneetbor / nich geneetbor

edible / inedible

böös / fründlich

evil / kind

fickerig / langwielt

excited / bored

dick / dünn

fat / thin

toeerst / toletzt

first / last

Fründ / Fiend

friend / enemy

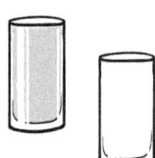

vull / leddig

full / empty

hart / week

hard / soft

swoor / licht

heavy / light

Smacht / Döst

hunger / thirst

krank / gesund

ill / healthy

nich na't Recht / na't Recht

illegal / legal

klook / dummerhaftig

intelligent / stupid

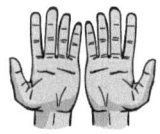

linkerhand / rechterhand

left / right

neeg / feern

near / far

nieg / bruukt
new / used

nix / wat
nothing / something

oolt / jung
old / young

an / ut
on / off

apen / slaten
open / closed

lies / luut
quiet / loud

riek / arm
rich / poor

richtig / verkehrt
right / wrong

ruug / glatt
rough / smooth

trurig / glücklich
sad / happy

kort / lang
short / long

suutje / flink
slow / fast

natt / dröög
wet / dry

warm / köhl
warm / cool

Krieg / Freden
war / peace

0

null
zero

1

een
one

2

twee
two

3

dree
three

4

veer
four

5

fief
five

6

söss
six

7

söven
seven

8

acht
eight

9

negen
nine

10

teihn
ten

11

ölven
eleven

12

twölf
twelve

13

dörteihn
thirteen

14

veerteihn
fourteen

15

föffteihn
fifteen

16

sössteihn
sixteen

17

söventeihn
seventeen

18

achtteihn
eighteen

19

negenteihn
nineteen

20

twintig
twenty

100

hunnert
hundred

1.000

dusend
thousand

1.000.000

million
million

Engelsch

English

Amerikaansch Engelsch

American English

Chineesch Mandarin

Chinese Mandarin

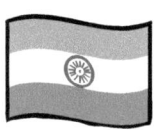

Hindi

Hindi

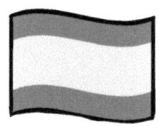

Spaansch

Spanish

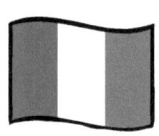

Franzöösch

French

Araabsch

Arabic

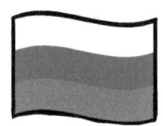

Rusch

Russian

Portugiesch

Portuguese

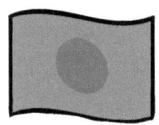

Bengaalsch

Bengali

Düütsch

German

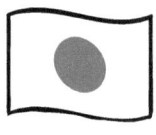

Japaansch

Japanese

ik

I

du

you

he / se / dat

he / she / it

wi

we

ji

you

se

they

keen?

who?

wat?

what?

woans?

how?

woneem?

where?

wannehr?

when?

Naam

name

where

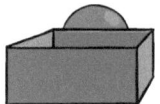

achter

behind

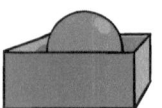

in

in

vör

in front of

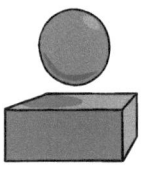

över

over

op

on

ünner

under

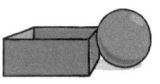

blangen

beside

twüschen

between

Oort

place